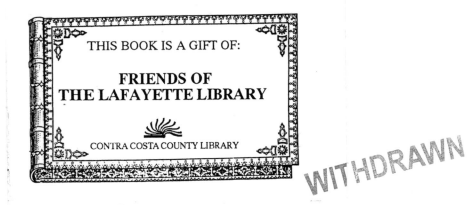

KIDS THROUGHOUT HISTORY ™

kids in the middle ages

Lisa A. Wroble

The Rosen Publishing Group's
PowerKids Press™
New York

Published in 1997 by The Rosen Publishing Group, Inc.
29 East 21st Street, New York, NY 10010

First Edition

Book Design: Danielle Primiceri

Photo Credits: Cover (left) provided by Archive Photos, (right) provided by Bettmann; p. 4 by Brueghel, provided by Bettmann; p. 7, provided by Bettmann; p. 8 by Brueghel the younger, provided by Bettmann; p. 11 by Jan Brueghel the elder, provided by Corbis-Bettmann; p. 12, provided by Corbis-Bettmann; p. 15 by Brueghel, provided by Corbis-Bettmann; p. 16 by J. Amman, provided by Archive Photos; p. 19, provided by Archive Photos; p. 20 by Pieter Brueghel, provided by Bettmann.

Wroble, Lisa A.
     Kids in the Middle Ages / Lisa A. Wroble.
          p.   cm. — (Kids throughout history)
     Includes index.
     Summary: Describes the life of a child during the Middle Ages, covering such aspects as food, clothing, housing, work, education, holidays, and religion.
     ISBN 0-8239-5120-0
     1. Civilization, Medieval—Juvenile literature. 2. Children—Europe—History—Juvenile literature. [1. Civilization, Medieval.] I. Title. II. Series: Wroble, Lisa A. Kids throughout history.
     GT120.W76
     305.23'094'0902—dc21   96-47239
                                                                                                  CIP
                                                                                                   AC

Manufactured in the United States of America

contents

the middle ages

the Middle Ages were a time in European history from about 500 A.D. to 1485 A.D. This time has been called the Middle Ages because some people believe they were the years between **ancient** (AYN-shent) and **modern** (MAH-dern) times. The church was very important to people during the Middle Ages. **Monks** (MUNKS) spent many hours writing and copying books that contained wisdom of ancient times. Their work was important for the great leaps in learning that came many years later.

Much of what we know today about life during the Middle Ages comes from the writing of monks.

lords and peasants

In the Middle Ages, cities grew near the castles of men called lords. A lord ruled over the people on his land the way a king rules over his kingdom. As cities grew, walls were built to protect the city from enemies. The land outside the city walls was used for farming. The people who farmed the land were called **peasants** (PEZ-ents). They gave the lord most of the food they grew for letting them use the land.

Peasant farmers worked hard. They had to grow enough food to feed their families and to please the lord. ▶

simon's village

Simon was a peasant boy in England. He lived in a **village** (VIL-ej) just outside one of the cities on his lord's land.

The streets of Simon's village were narrow. The houses were built close together. The main road through Simon's village led from his lord's manor to the nearest church. Simon's house was about half-way between the manor and the church. There were no streetlights during the Middle Ages, so it was very dark at night. Simon carried a lantern when he walked home after working in the fields all day.

Life in villages like Simon's centered on the community of people who lived there.

9

a peasant home

Simon's house was made of wood. The roof was made of tightly woven grass called **thatch** (THACH). There was one room downstairs. It had a **hearth** (HARTH) where Simon's mom built fires to cook and to keep warm during the winter. Simon and his family ate their meals at a big wooden table in front of the hearth. A ladder led upstairs, where there were two small rooms: one for Simon and the other for his parents. Each room had a stool for sitting and a straw-filled sack on which to sleep.

Most meals were cooked in one big kettle over an open fire. ▶

farming

Simon got up early every day to help his family work in the fields. Simon's family grew wheat, oats, hay, turnips, and other vegetables. They, and all the other peasants, had to give most of the food they grew to the people living in the manor.

The lord owned all the land and all the animals living on the land. Simon and his father were not allowed to hunt or fish unless the lord said they could.

Most peasant children didn't go to school. They helped their families in the fields.

clothing

imon and his father wore **tunics** (TOO-niks) made from wool. They wore loose pants called **breeches** (BRIT-chez). Sometimes they wore long stockings instead, or wrapped their legs with long strips of cloth. Over their tunics they wore a sleeveless cape called a **surcoat** (SIR-koht). Simon's mother wore a longer tunic that looked like a loose dress. On her head she wore a hood with a veil that draped across her throat. This was called a **wimple** (WIM-pul). Simon's mother made most of the clothes her family wore.

The clothes that peasants wore were usually made at home. ▶

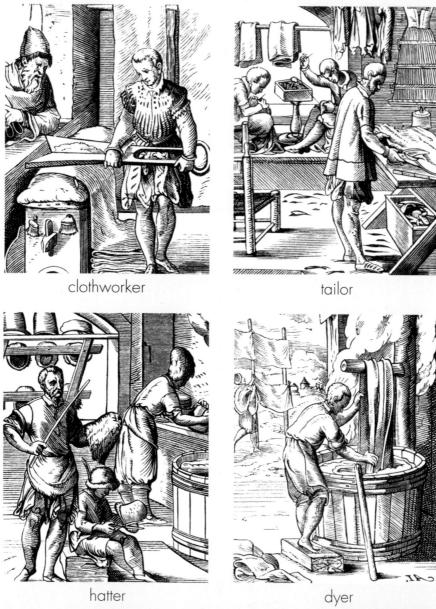

clothworker

tailor

hatter

dyer

WORKING AND LEARNING

most people in the Middle Ages didn't learn to read or write. Only boys who would become church leaders went to school. Some boys, like Simon, worked in the fields. Other boys learned special skills by working as **apprentices** (uh-PREN-tis-sez). They worked with someone who knew how to do a job, such as a blacksmith, a potter, or a shoemaker. Some kids were chosen to work in the lord's manor. Boys usually took care of the horses. Girls often worked in the kitchen, helping to cook and clean.

◄ *As apprentices, some boys learned how to make or dye cloth, sew clothes, and make hats.*

the black death

People in the Middle Ages didn't know that keeping clean was a good way to stay healthy. They didn't take baths or clean their clothes very often. Piles of garbage lined the streets. Rats ate the garbage. The rats had fleas that spread a **disease** (dih-ZEEZ) across Europe. It was called the **bubonic plague** (byoo-BON-ik PLAYG), and it killed millions of people. It caused black spots to appear on people's bodies. Because of the spots, it was also called the Black Death.

Doctors in the Middle Ages didn't know how to help people who had the bubonic plague. ▶

the church

uring the Middle Ages, people relied heavily on church leaders to guide them through life. Church leaders explained the teachings of the church and the way they believed the world worked through stories in the Bible. The church was responsible for the most beautiful art and architecture of this time. The huge **cathedrals** (kuh-THEE-drulz) that were built and the stained glass windows that were made showed how strongly people felt about their religion. The 1,000 years of the Middle Ages were a time in which people knew their place in their community and in the world.

holy days

t he **Christian** (KRIS-chen) church was a big part of Simon's life. Everyone, from the peasants to the lords, went to church on Sundays and other holy days.

The peasants worked hard. But they also had fun on holy days. After going to church they ate, sang, and danced in the village. At Christmas the lord held a feast at the manor and often invited the peasants to come.

◀ *The people of the Middle Ages worked hard in the fields. But on holy days they ate well and had fun.*

GLOSSARY

ancient (AYN-shent) A very long time ago.

apprenctice (uh-PREN-tis) Young person learning a skill or trade.

breeches (BRIT-chez) Loose pants that were fastened at the knee.

bubonic plague (byoo-BON-ik PLAYG) Fatal illness spread by the fleas that lived on rats.

Christian (KRIS-chen) Someone who believes in Jesus Christ.

cathedral (kuh-THEE-drul) A large church in which important church leaders worked.

disease (dih-ZEEZ) Sickness.

hearth (HARTH) Stone or brick floor of a fireplace.

modern (MAH-dern) Of the present time, beginning around 1485 A.D.

monk (MUNK) A man who belongs to a religious order and lives in a house connected to a church called a monastery.

peasant (PEZ-ent) Farmer in Europe in the Middle Ages.

surcoat (SIR-koht) Sleeveless outercoat.

thatch (THACH) Dried straw or grass woven into thick sheets.

tunic (TOO-nik) Large, loose shirt.

village (VIL-ej) During the Middle Ages, a small town on a lord's land.

wimple (WIM-pul) A veil that covers the throat.

index